My Happy Easter Book

Matthew 27:57–28:10 for Children

Written by Gloria A. Truitt
Illustrated by Len Ebert

ARCH ® Books
Copyright © 1996 Concordia Publishing House
3558 S. Jefferson Avenue, St. Louis, MO 63118-3968
Manufactured in the United States of America

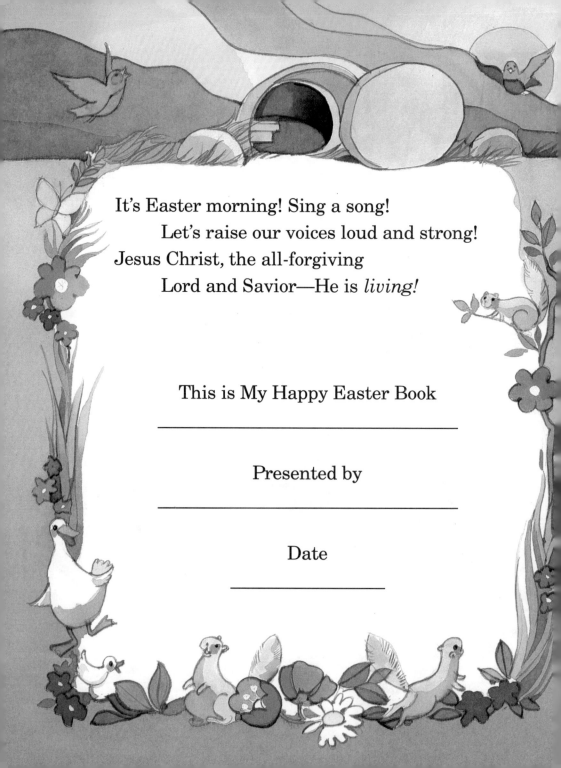

It's Easter morning! Sing a song!
Let's raise our voices loud and strong!
Jesus Christ, the all-forgiving
Lord and Savior—He is *living!*

This is My Happy Easter Book

_____

Presented by

_____

Date

_____

When Jesus died upon the cross,
His friends looked on and cried;
For they had lost their Master,
Their Lord and loving Guide.

A friend wrapped Jesus' body in
Fine linens; then he laid
Our Lord within his family tomb—
A cave that he had made.

To make sure no one could go in,
He rolled a giant stone
Across the entrance; then he left.
Now Jesus was alone.

While Jesus suffered on the cross,
    Two women watched nearby.
They both were grieving for their Lord,
    And, oh, how they did cry.

Both women were called Mary, and
    They loved the Lord, you see.
So, two days later they were filled
    With curiosity.

Toward the tomb they rushed with speed.
They had to take a look!
All at once an earthquake struck!
Imagine how they shook!

Then suddenly God's angel came
And rolled the stone away!
"Don't be afraid," the angel said.
"Come see where Jesus lay."

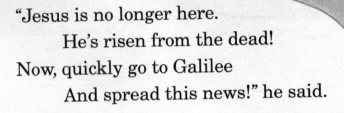

"Jesus is no longer here.
　　He's risen from the dead!
Now, quickly go to Galilee
　　And spread this news!" he said.

Before they left, the women looked
　　Where Jesus had been placed.
Then overjoyed they said, "Let's run!
　　There is no time to waste!"

So the women hurried off—
　　Their hearts were filled with gladness!
"It must be true! He lives again!"
　　No longer they felt sadness.

Then suddenly the women met
Their Savior on the way!
"Greetings!" Jesus said to them
On that first Easter day.

The women ran to Him and knelt
Before Him on the ground;
Then clasped His feet and worshiped Him—
Their Savior had been found!

Jesus said, "Don't be afraid!
Now go to Galilee
And tell My faithful followers
That there they will see Me!"

Purple stands for royalty,
    In case you didn't know,
Because the kings wore purple robes
    In days of long ago.

When Jesus was on trial that day—
    That day so sad and grim—
The folks who hated Jesus placed
    A purple robe on Him.

They yelled, "King of the Jews!" and laughed
    While making cruel fun.
How sad they didn't recognize
    Our Savior as God's Son.

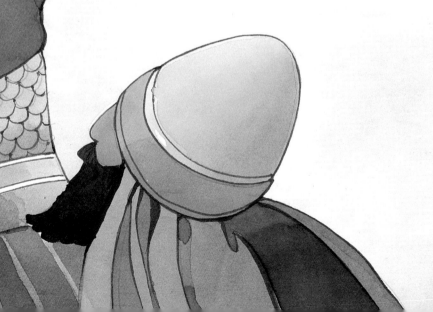

The color white means clean and pure.
 That's what the angel wore
When he rolled away the stone
 That blocked the Lord's tomb door!

The joyous time of Easter comes
　　Always during the spring
When, following the winter's chill,
　　We hear the robins sing.

Now everywhere we look it seems
　　That fresh, new life is seen—
From budding trees to crawly worms,
　　And many sprouts of green.

Praise God for it is wonderful
That Jesus came to earth,
Then died, but rose to live again,
So *we* could have new birth!

Think of all the colors that
    You see at Easter time.
Then use them on the lines below
    To make up your own rhyme!

My Easter Poem

_____

_____

_____

_____

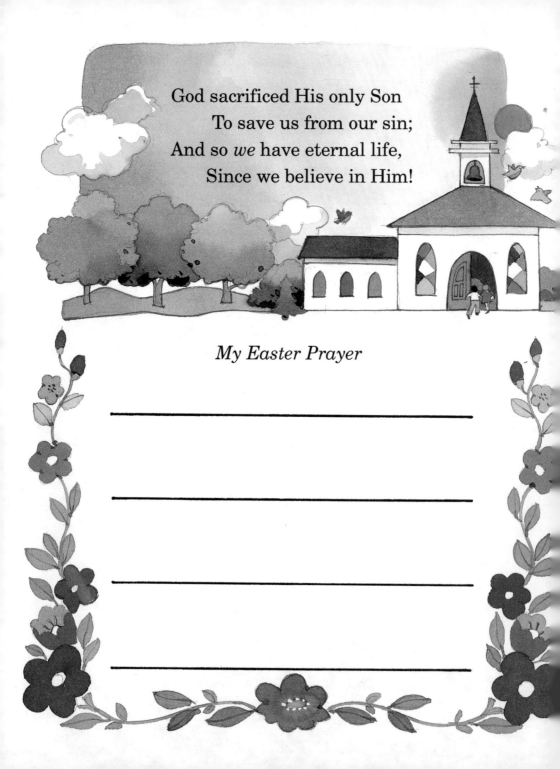

God sacrificed His only Son
   To save us from our sin;
And so *we* have eternal life,
   Since we believe in Him!

My Easter Prayer

_____

_____

_____

_____